Art of life

Uparima Goonetillake

Art of Life

Dedications

To my father, Prins Gunasekara,
with eternal gratitude

And

To all those sublime souls
in search of peace, joy and love

Contents

Acknowledgements

Many thanks to Kaijoumari for all the invaluable help, encouragement, and support in publishing my first book.

I also acknowledge with appreciation the guidance and advice offered by Mala Shirani.

My friends and family have been instrumental in my journey and adding colours and flavours to my life.

My teachers have been many, and although some of the best life lessons have been the toughest, I am grateful for it all.

The wisest of souls have touched my life with their magic, love and endless wisdom.

If I can imbibe some of that into my own life, then I could repay them for all that they have been to me.

Thank you....

Come take a walk with me
Down life's green pathways
Sometimes you might meet the roses
Something the thorns

Smile and wave and bid them farewell
But most of all
Enjoy the walk

Something wonderful is happening

Right here, right now

The unfolding of a bud

The unravelling of a mystery

The opening of a heart and mind
Understanding of a special kind

Let us all imagine

Into being

A brand new world

Filled with

Love and peace

For everyone

When there are billions of thoughts to choose

from, lets choose some good ones today...

Who knows, we might even end

up with some great ones

To love trees

Trees.. they breathe life in to us

Provide us the essential and the non-essential

All those books, throughout the years

The beauty and the grace

The comfort and the support

A friend you can find anywhere

Except perhaps in the desert

And a love that lasts a lifetime

With Gratitude

Sometimes all you need
Is a little nudge
To help you fly
Above the clouds

To help you soar
And reach heights
You never imagined
Even existed

Sometimes all you need
Is a little help
And waving of
A magic wand

With Gratitude

With much gratitude to all those who nudge and help

Don't say a word, for volumes are spoken in silence....

The Mighty One

Looking into your deep blue
My soul awakened
Touched by your gentle strength
I found my own

Under the roar of your mighty power
I could hear the whisper of my own self

Connecting with your all-encompassing love
I found the truth of my own being

I brought all my troubles to you
And you took them all away

Thank you
For your grace and ease
The flow that never ceases
And caresses our hearts
Solaces our souls
Washes away all the pain
In your mighty endless compassion

Love

It started with a tree
Then the mountains
Next the ocean
And that just about
Covered the whole world
My love

Blasting barriers

Blast the barriers to love
Incinerate the roadblocks to your heart
Dynamite a clear path
And you find happiness flowing in
Dancing around with glee
Shouting from the rooftop,
'I am in love'...

You will go wandering around
With a smile on your face
And tears of joy
running down your face
Sweetness beyond reason
Ecstasy beyond this realm

And Delight in everything
Mumbling like a fool
Madly in love
Again….

The Unknowing

In the darkness

Stumbling and falling
Feeling my away around
Hardly knowing
When or where

But somehow made it
Through it all.

Tears for a child

Baby these tears are for you
The lost and lonely child
Unsure about everything
Most of all, unsure about oneself

Will anyone care for me?
Am I worthy?
Why did love leave so fast
Never to come back again?

Let these tears be the last shed
For I will keep you safe
I will take care of you
And love you forever and a day....

Eight hours and a half

Eight hours and a half
That's how long it took me
To wake up
The dream is strong
Its clutches considerable
What is beyond is largely hidden
The tears in the veil
Give glimpse into the future
One that is brighter, softer, gentler and kinder

Break free from the clutches of the fantasy
And let the dreamer find its freedom..
The greener pasture, the rolling mountains
And the bright blue ocean, all in one...

Unconditional love for oneself is the most important achievement in our lives

You on my mind

Life the school of hard knocks
You can bounce back higher,
The harder you hit the ground
Thus take the bees sting with the honey
And dance all the way
To the bank

You are loved

A certain sweetness, happiness came in
Sat down beside me
Comforted me, kept me company
Held my hand, kissed my hair
And said, You are loved....

Lift lift
lift me up
Up, up and away

Lift lift
sometimes take me
down
Down down
down
sometimes take me
down
to catch the train

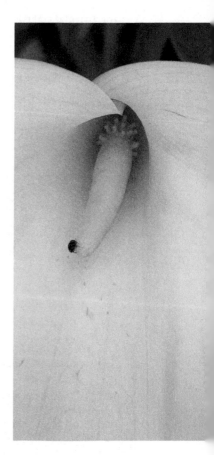

I am

I am a leaf hanging on the branch
A dew drop waiting for the sun
A mist covering the mountain side
I am I said

I am a girl singing a song
Dancing away before a stature
A raindrop falling on the parched earth
I am, I am

I am a dream waking up
A lamp in the darkness
A minute frozen in time
I am and I will be

Joy

Joy you bring
Manna from heaven

Peace unquenchable
Lilies from the valley

Fairy dust so we can
soar

Joy you bring
Choice in every moment

Golden sunsets
Blue heavens

The freedom to fly
above
the clouds....

Je sais Je suis

In the middle of the night
When I know of nothing
Where, when , how why or where-upon
I know nothing
Except that I am

If I can still my mind
Till I can hear the melting of the ice caps
And the curdling of the milk
I know that I breath
I know I am

I know nothing about you
Where, when, how, whence and wherefore
And there is no way of knowing
I can leave all the longing to know
And breath deep as
I know, I am

Time flies on turbo
boost wings
Tarry a while
Slow down please
So I could catch you
Hold you
For a brief moment

"To set your life on fire seek those who fan your flames."
~ Rumi

The day beckons me,
the night will not let me be,
come on,
there is much to be done,
many places to go, things to be.
It is only 3am, I beseech, but it will not
listen to reason.
A clear question imposes - open your
eyes, what can you see?

Holding on tight

In the middle of the night

In the darkness I reach out

My soul keeps me company

Holding on tight

Whispering sweet nothings

Gentle calm words of love

Gentle warm waves of compassion

A single bright star

An endless promise

Of support,

Sweet

Kind

I can breath again

With you

"When I let go of who I am,
I become what I might be."
~ Lao Tzu

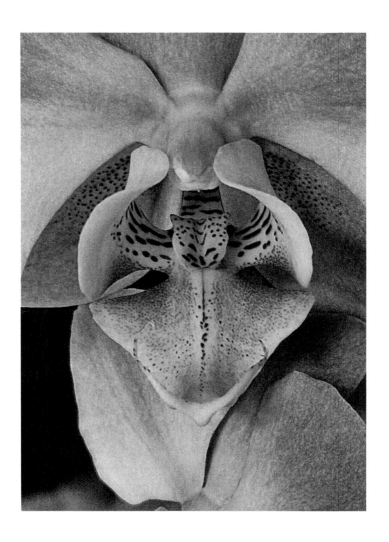

When You

When you look into my soul
I feel a resounding Yeah
A joy bubbles up
And grapples with my heart
Come play with me
Be my sweetheart
For in your love
I have found myself
For in your tears
I have drowned myself
Walk gently my love
For the rose petals of my heart
Are scattered at your feet
Beauty nudges me from all sides
As bliss cascades down my spine
A resounding Yeah
When you look into my soul
And all this
With just one look
When you look into my soul

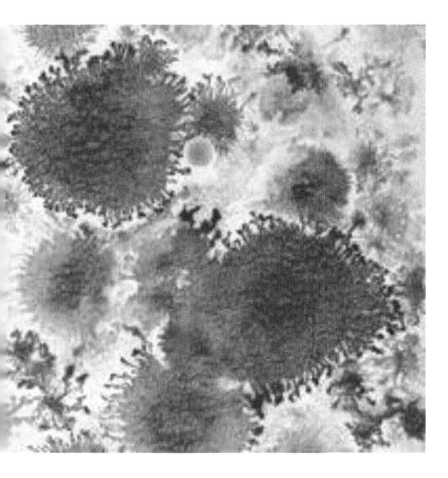

"Imagination is everything.
It is the preview of life's
coming attractions." ~Albert
Einstein

Adequate

It is enough
That the stars come out only at night
The mist hangs out at dawn and on
Some very fortunate nights

It is enough
That the birds sing their chorus
And the rain falls sometimes
But not on every parched ground

It is enough
That you sit by my side sometime
Share your dreams with me
And talk to me softly of love

"The quieter you become,
the more you are able to hear."
— Rumi

O Peace….!!

Knock knock
Who has the key
To open the door
To a gentler world
Where peace abides
Love reigns above all
The dove's soft coo
Brings forth joy and delight
Flowers bloom
To greet the sun
The trees whisper
A lover's dream
A single ray of the moon
Kisses the face in ecstasy

When peace abides

Who?

Who is there

Tapping at my window

Clearing the snow from my path

Keeping me company

Day and night

Who is it

That rings my bell

Writing me notes

Reminders

Someone there

Watching over me

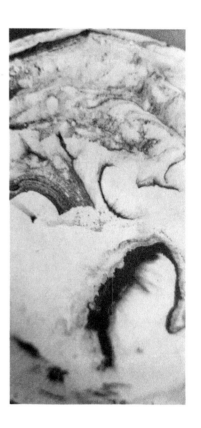

Who would think highly of lessons of love
learnt in the midst of warfare?

Strange Universe, Doctor

Smashed and broken,
But still ticking
All you have to do
Is replace the glass

Then it is as good as new
Perhaps even better
For who knows,
Maybe it's the broken heart
That withstands the mightiest winds
And stands unshaken
Before all its fears
And builds the world up
From the start
Something New
Something Worthwhile
Something Grand

Gentle

Walk gently
For the clamour
Of the tin cans
Tied to your ankles
Make a mighty
Big Noise

The sea

I long for the sea
With a longing so strong
It crashes on the shores of my soul
Reverberating and Echoing
Throughout all eternity

A longing that drowns out everything
Until nothing else is left
A deep deep longing
Burning a hole in my being
Turning my mind to cinders
That lay scattered like dust
Tiny swirling eddies
At my feet

Let me count my blessing

The dew drop on the rose petal
The golden hues of the setting sun
Waves that crash against my soul
Salt water on my mind
A bird that sings me a love song
A parrot so green and gay
A parasol of unlimited colours
A sad song on a rainy day
A blush on the cheeks of a young lass
Merrily on her way
Butterflies that wink at me
Night caps to keep me warm
Gentle hands and kind hearts
And smiles of abundant joy
Oh, so many are the blessings,
I have lost count on the way……

- "There are more things in Heaven and Earth, Horatio, than are dreamt of in your philosophy."

- — William Shakespeare, Hamlet

Fall in Love

Fall in love every day
Just a little bit more
With the wind and the sky
and the clouds and the rain

With the red berries that glisten and shine
With the barn owl and the cockroach
The lame excuses that fall on deaf ears
The gentle voices that plead for mercy

Among the deafening screeching of the parakeets
With life with all its beauty and complexity
With roses that scream for attention and love
With tears blue and round that resounds
as it hits the ground

With teacups and supper bowls
With red dresses and gaudy balls
With wine that trickle down the alleyways
And leave red stains on my clothes
But more than that, on every day
Fall in love with your own self….

Triggers

At the touch of a button,

you come to mind....

Now, where is that button,

and why does it trigger so much?

Is it something you told me a long long time ago,

When love was new a

Like a butter green leaf

At the start of spring

Or Is it a promise

That insists on

Not being broken?

A turtle

A turtle asked me a question one day
What would you be if you could be anything
Anything at all
I gazed into his smiling eyes and replied
I would be you, all of you

Riches

If you are rich, why beg at the doors of heaven?

If you have cloaks of velvet, why drape yourself in tatters?

If you have everything, why cry over what is lost?

For, when you check your pockets, you find, you have never lost what is truly yours

The key was always in your hand

Velvet and gold were your constant companions

Just because the clouds hid it, the sun was still shining

It is just that you could not see

How very loved you are.....

Dream Dragons

Dreams and Dangers mingle
On the show of broken promises
Dangling on the edge of the precipice
We are all puppets on a string

Trying yet failing
Does it make any sense at all?
Or are we all dancing
To the beat of a distant drum?

The silent shadows
Dance on the wall
Preying on the imaginations
To add spice or terror

A question of free will
A question of choice
Or are we just dangling
Just one puppet at a time?

You push me away
Until I want to run away
Screaming in pain
From the top of my lungs

Be myself

Ah, to be myself,
On a magical rainy day
Just nothing else to do,
But be myself
I can hear the angels sing
The cupids clasp their hands in glee
The butterflies flutter by
Shouting three cheers all the way
The crows clamour in glee
Just to see this happy sight
The bluebells nod their heads
In agreement and delight
Ah, what a sight indeed
I, just being myself…..

"Live in the present, launch yourself on every wave, find eternity in each moment."
~ Henry David Thoreau

"When the violin can forgive the past it starts singing. When the violin can stop worrying about the future, it will become such a drunk laughing nuisance that God will then lean down and start combing you into his hair. When the violin can forgive every wound caused by others, the heart starts singing."

~ Hafiz

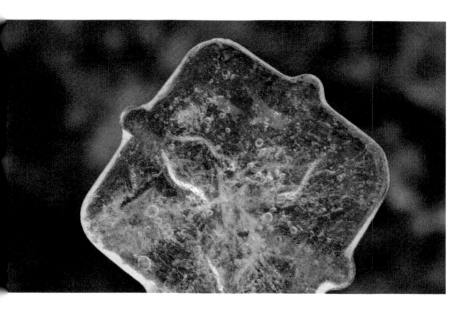

The pain crusts over

Until another scratch takes the scab away

Red mixes blue where you hurt me

But when you hold me,

It all dissolves into the ether

Like we walked a different path and

Lived a different life

It is amazing how amazing you are.....

Freedom

When my heart escapes the clutches of the earth
And flies tossing with the birds
Dances among the moonbeams and
Swirls with the setting sun

Dream forever among the stars
Scream in glee from the top of the voice
I am free, free from turmoil
Forever free

The mist hung heavy on that magical day...
you entered my life

"There is a tide in the affairs of men
Which, taken at the flood, leads on to fortune"

— William Shakespeare , Julius Caesar

Seven hundred and nineteen

Seven hundred and nineteen degrees Celsius
The temperature at which the heart bursts into flame
The ashes swirl around in little eddies
Helpless little children crying out for their mothers
When the gates are locked and bolted
And we have nowhere else to go
All calls for help are futile
And the exit point no more
No matter what you believe in
The temples are crashing down around you
The fallen idols lay scattered, covered in sin
Shame, Guilt, Fear, Anger, Hopelessness
And our broken voices lamenting the loss
of innocence
The eyes do not see what lies beyond
The horror, the tears, the golden flames
A thin layer covers all the senses
Until the day of redemption
Unrequited love and a vendetta
Lies buried six feet under the snow
Yet the moon smiles in amusement
Why can't you see, how much you are loved
And the stars sing in unison,
We will give you all you want
Beings made of stardust
We are all worthy
and somehow, very enough
Finally, a lullaby drifting from way beyond
Puts the restless children to sleep

Grateful
Look up at the sky
Bow down low
Giving thanks
For everything

You define love
in so many ways
and in all its guises
You tell me how much
You love me

Autumn leaf

A falling leaf binds me to the moment
Peace abounds in the here and now

The slow dance as it reaches to kiss the earth
Like keeping an eternal promise to oneself

You and I are one
The briefest time
When we were apart
Is surely coming to an end
Let the wind whisper its sweet secrets to me,
But to you my lord, I will surely return

Do not be fooled by the slowness of my dance
For I, belong to you, forever…

Longing for love

One thousand years of longing
to look up and see the sky
freedom, who knows where it started
Who knows where it will end
Hope, like an endless kite tail
Bobbin in the wind,
Nodding yes yes yes
One day, it will happen,
One day, you will see
The blue light
of love

Day Dreams are made of these
A touch, a look
Longing stare out of the
window
I could wait a lifetime
For a reply, a sign
That you saw me too.....

Misery

Misery loves company
Come sit by my side,
it whispered softly
stay a while
and listen to my story
It is a tale of woe
woven with grief
painted with sorrow
washed with tears
emptied of meaning
However,
I would love you to
come sit with me
just for the shortest while
and shed a tear or two
with me

Allowing the wonder

Allowing
The dreams
The passion
The love
Even the shadows
The darkness
The kindness in the night
Allowance
Allowance
Opening the doors to
Gratitude
Pain
Feeling
Jealousy
Madness
That trickle down slowly
Like honey
Dripping down
One drop after another
Sweet, sticky, insane

Preference

Do you prefer tea or coffee?
I prefer a mansion

Why offer me things of small stature?
I would like somewhere I could live in forever

One step forward

One step forward
Two steps back
One step forward
Two steps back
What are you terrified of, little mouse?
I don't know,
A shadow screamed at me
A noise startled me
And around the corner
I hear,
The shattering of my soul
The light might flicker off
The tide might turn
And we all could end up dead
In the middle of the night

Mourning

It drops cold
Like condensed dew on a frosty morning
Still, like in the dead of the night
On a windless frozen times
Nothings shifts
Hearts broken, mended over time
Tears shed, no more now
With a smile on our lips
We celebrate
A life well lived
A journey of love
Everlasting
May your heart find peace
That would never leave
May your memory bring smiles
For ever more….
Go gently into the night
With your fierce, loving soul……

My greatest gift ever

You flutter with my breath
And hide behind every heartbeat
My little butterfly...you...
Your mighty pawprints are all over my heart

May the wind carry every sigh
And the sky bear witness to every heartache
The earth carry my burden and my pain
So you never ever need to see me cry

Peace

To choose joy is to do yourself a favour
So choose joy every minute if you can
And if enough of us did that
There would be no more room for war
Find that piece of peace in our hearts
And keep it there for all
So there will be no more
No more need for war

Who

Who can ask for love?
An Adorable dog?
A broken child?
A tear frozen in eternity?

A cute puppy gets all the love
The blazing sun gets all the adoration
The gentle moon need not ask for love

However, what about the broken?
The dispossessed?
The black sheep of the family?

Can they ask for love
Or should they simply sit in a corner
To whimper and lick their wounds?

I could swim in your eyes and drown in your love, so vast and colossal it is..

SHINE A TORCH ON THE
SHADOWS, SO THEY
LONGER SCARE YOU.

Thank you for the love

Thank you for the stories
woven by the moonlight
touched by magic
falling at my feet
shining pearls of hardened tears
Cascading through the years
Building momentum
Unravelling the mysteries
of untold past and futures
Would you tell me one more story
One more whisper
Before the moon dips
Behind the mountain?

Thank you for the love

I can still hear
the echoes
the tap tap tap
of those pearls falling
as they hit the ground

I don't know who I am, but it is enough, to love
this unknown person….

I don't know who You are
either, but it is also enough,
just to love this unknown
person….

Thank you for the love

Thank you for the faith, the love
Thank you for the belief and the love
For helping me to weave
The fabric of my life
The shimmering shades
The delicate gold
that magical storyline
spiralling through the ages
Can we write
one more story together
Whisper one more time
So I remember
How it used to be????

IT IS

A love triangle - I, myself and me - and know what???
I think it could work very well....
dancing smiling hugging and cuddling....all three of us
together...I love myself, myself loves me and me loves
I...........

The Jester vs. The Joke

Lightning strikes, though my heart
Ripping it apart
Facing the dangers of the night
I still stand, upright
When the clown comes to call us,
we all need to go,
Singing, dancing, joking,
Skipping, right to the end
Strange things happen
In the dark
Eyes meet eyes
clasping in the moonlight
Like nobody's business
Like the end
Should never come
When we hold each other
Like this
What is it that I feel
is it love, is it, is it
Fingers reaching out,
Making contact,
Fading in the dusk
Like particles of air
That never saw the light
Shining, shimmering
Yet, here, now....

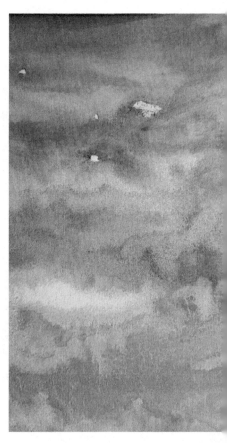

Hold my hand and you don't need to let it go

Your fierce love
I will remember forever
And be ever grateful for

When you are in love, it feels good to be close to the focus of affections.

Clear and Clouded

Nothing is clear except my heart
 the insistent echoes throughout its chambers
Lay bare the roots...

Why is my heart like an egg
On a tightrope?
Precariously balanced
A grand fall any moment

Unknot, unknot unknot
unlock and let it go
For at the end of the rainbow
Lies a bucket filled with
Promises, nay, better still, Freedom

Enough is not even a definition but I am happy to bargain with it, for the sake of my sanity

"Wear gratitude like a cloak and it will feed

every corner of your life."

-Rumi

If all you can do is stand there, that is good enough.

And I will stand here and be happy with where you are....

Ghosts from the past

When the ghosts of the past,
Not having been laid to rest
Creep up on you
And scare you with a loud 'Boo'
You jump out of your skin
And start running a mile

All because of a ghost
From the past
Came a-calling....

Can we finally lay them to rest?

Today is another day

I plan to be happy today. Just for today..

For tomorrow can look after itself

And let the past keep its secrets and its misery

The future can keep its problems and anxieties

Just for today, be happy

Good Habits

Love
Focusing on the good
Gratitude
Kindness
Compassion towards
 oneself and others
Smiling
Skipping along merrily

Just love a little bit more, just a tiny winy little bit more....
For maybe in the grand scheme of things
That would be all that really matters
Love a little, give a little, ask for a little bit more
Sing a little, dance a little
Kiss a little bit more

Why is my heart stuck at capital letters, screaming at the top of my lungs, hoping you will hear me?

Total Strangers

My head is spinning
My body is dancing
I wonder where I will lay
At the end of all this

Confusion around
A mist is rolling
Oh, is that someone I know
It very well might be

Look in the mirror to see the real you
For the reflection paints a more authentic picture

Ode to a beautiful lady

Talking to you makes me feel so human
Like your smile can switch on a love button
In my heart
Bubbles of joy crawling up my spine
They will not be denied
They will not be denied
Is it simply because
I spoke to you?
And your kindness seeped through?

A beautiful smile and a beautiful heart
Can make all the difference
In the whole world!!!

Clouds

Random clouds
Across the sky
Painting a billion pictures
Wonder what it means
A dragon or a fairy godmother
A monster or a dog
Who can tell???
Only our imagination....

Speak to me softly of love, my precious, so i may know what the eyes cannot see...

Look at me

Look at me look at me look at me
Look how I dance
Look how I sing
Look how I look

You like it or not
You love it or hate
You smile or frown
It doesn't much matter

This is just the way I am
And somehow, it is good enough

Your judgement does not need
to live in my world

Opening up to a new possibility
Every day, a new chance
Even if everything is lost
We can still look up
Seek the light, with new hope
And a simple Thank You!!!!

Needs and Wants

My life has been full of conflict, for as long as I remember, both within and without.

But fighting for what I wanted or what I thought was right did not bring it into being

Now I want to move away from conflict, as I see the futility of it in my life.

Perhaps there is another way to build a new tomorrow.

Perhaps that way is to build a new moment NOW.

Away from conflict, away from trying, away from asking or begging or looking for it.

Perhaps just sit with what I want, in silence and feel its presence into being.

This, I feel, is the way forward for me.

Peace, Love and Joy

Declutter

Declutter, declutter declutter....
My brains out...
Never mind the wardrobe

Beauty

One day soon, I will be beautiful too
When the rain hits the ground
And the parched cracks heal up
One day soon, I will be beautiful too

One day soon, I will be smiling, too
When the perfumed rose yields its glory
To the setting sun
One day soon....

One day soon, I will wipe the tears away
When the new moon rises
And greets me with love
And wipe all my tears away, for me....

Why Why

It doesn't matter so much
What you see
As how you see
Beauty and all its interpretations
Exclusively created in our minds

A clear heart and rose-tinted glasses
Will keep your spirits high
Help you skip along with joy
In your mind....

Give and take

Can I count all that you have given me
My life, my riches, my mind and my strength
To stand on my two feet
Feel the ground beneath me shift
And still keep standing

To love and feel love
Under the hardest of circumstances
Not keel under the pressure
Of immense burdens unbearable

Still keep going and going and going
Even when all seems lost
And the end of the tunnel
Looks like a big black hole

We all have the power
To withstand all adversity
To keep standing, despite the swaying
And keep counting our blessings

Apple of my eye

That day you took a bite from
my heart
And crippled me for life
Next day we went to the
supermarket
Had our photos taken.
Even otherwise,
I could not forget that day
You took a big bite...
From my heart

"Doubt thou the stars are fire;
Doubt that the sun doth move;
Doubt truth to be a liar;
But never doubt I love."
— William Shakespeare, Hamlet

Sing and dance, like the flowers do, to the beat of that distant drum

The perfect imperfection

Look at me with all my imperfections
Judge if you must
However, it is alright
For I accept myself
And all your judgements
Will not change the way
I see myself
All the judgements
Will not make me feel
Any less adequate
Any less worthy
Or something about me has to change
For me to be Enough.
For I am good enough, as I stand.

Wherefore

All the things I dream of
in the middle of the night
 I obsess over you
Why where how when,
wherefore art thou not with me?

The fire eating dragon
Is in love with me

We hold hands
And she sets me on fire
My world burns
Turning into ashes
Arming the hot clouds
I moan for the losses

Do speak to me often
So that I may know
What and where and how
You came to be

Vegas Nerve

I drop my head to one side
And stare at the other corner
I start to feel better already
Like you touched me
Ever so gently
On a cold and windy day
And the cobwebs in my mind
Swirl around and fly away
Like never to come back again
And the heavy lifts
Like a bird of prey grabbed it
From my heart
To fly away far far away
To feed it to the little chicks
Perched on a clifftop
Hope it doesn't give them
Indigestion....

Drunk on life, a splatter of colour drops on the canvas of creation, making its mark. Who created this masterpiece other than the pulsating desire for beauty and completion?

Among the roses

Something sublime this way comes
Suddenly your heart is trapped
A prisoner of the awe that surrounds
All the senses
Come and say you will sing my song
And we can journey the rest of the way
Holding hands
among the roses

Gratitude

Eternal and all encompassing
Just like your love for me

Thank you for being everything to me
All the love, all the support all the comfort

I felt it in my being
In my body and in my soul

It was always returned fully
Mother Nature......

No thing

Nothing makes sense
Everything make sense
At the same time

Magical

Something Magical
About you
Made me reach out
And touch you

Something beautiful
Called to my heart
Interlinked our lives
With a thread of gold

Fancy that?
Just a brief encounter
That spoke volumes
Brought a smile
To our live

Perhaps our heart
Were inextricably linked
Or just the magic in you
Spoke to the magic in me...?

Ah

Ah what a privilege
To be myself
To Be myself
To Be myself

I lived a whole life
through
Just for the one
chance
To be myself
A privilege of a
lifetime
No less

Sit

All the way to the back
All the way to the back
Sit there
Sit there
Make way for others
Lest we forget
To think of others
Brothers in arms
Holding each other
To the end
Till death do us part

Friend from the rock

Your plight touched me
When you said the rains washed your walls away
And you spend most night,
Trying to stop the rain
From flooding the house
Repairing the roof,
All by your self

A woman like any other
By a giant by any standard
My friend from the rock
Thank you for noticing
My smile….

It was indeed
Fate that brought us together

Evening tide...

Sacred moments joined together with silken threads, where you can close your eyes and simply slip into the warmth of those comforting familiar assured peace and tranquillity.

Bond street

Yet again we meet
So close yet so far away

In the darkness as I lie
And think of you
The river flows outside
In the dusky unknown
In the pitch black
No one can see
Just like my love for you
That no one can see....

Grateful for the birds that fly,
Soaring high above
Taking my heart with you
On the wings of freedom

Control

The main thing that needs control
Is our thoughts,
Not the outside
Or other people
If our thoughts are in our control
So will our emotions be

And these are the building blocks
Of our lives

Not other people
Or outside situations
Just our thoughts,
Just our thoughts...

My relationship with you is much better
As my relationship with myself is much better

Blessings

Can I count you
once?

Twice?

Nay, many many
many times...

For you define

The word Blessing

In so many many
many ways....

Thank You

For no matter how you touched me
You rebirthed me
Made me who I am
Made me remember
Made me smile
With myself
For the secrets of life
Lie in the sand
You just need to shift them
Just a tiny bit
To read everything
And to know
For yourself
All there is to know
So thank you
For being there for me....

I cannot make you happy
You cannot make me happy
That is totally up to each other

Would love by any other name smell as sweet?
Perhaps it could....

The Blue Green

A vista of green blue heaven

Surrounds

The value of

Perfectly still serenity

A mirage of great importance

The mountains stand tall

Full of light reflections

The sea

Whispering its secrets to anyone

Who reaches its shores

Pulsating, Pushing, towards understanding

And a Peace beyond all comprehension

A peace that knows no reason

And asks for nothing in return

The resonance from the depth of our
sorrow to the heights of our bliss,
inspires and aids the creative process
and colours the fabric of our art

Never mind the rain

Oh Scary, when the rain falls down
When the shoes don't fit
And the days do bark
Secrets fall to the ground
With a resounding thud

Never mind the rain
Or the barking day
Endless dark nights
Without any lights
But oh the secrets
They run through my fingers
Trying to escape
A mind of their own
Knocking on the door
In the dead of the night
Ringing the bells,
Asking for permission
To be heard...
For redemption....and release....

You

You didn't let me
drown

It must be love

You didn't let me
down

It must be love

You

The Eternal Joker

Trying to tease a smile

Out of the Universe

Trying to ease the pain

With a wink

A blank stare

A secret glare

A hidden twist

To the endless tale

Dance with me

A step or two

Enjoy the ride

For its only for a while

Or perhaps

An eternity?

More more more

Can I have

a little bit more

Just a tiny bit more

What's wrong

With whining

And asking

For just

a little bit more?

Questions

You cannot
understand

Or

you will not
understand

That is the question

Meet the Author
Uparima Goonetillake

Uparima Goonetillake is a poet and
an artist originally from Sri Lanka,
who is currently based in London.

Her work explores the complexities
of the human experience
and the beauty that can be found within it.

She often incorporates both
poetry and art into her pieces,
resulting in a unique and
thought-provoking blend
of the two mediums.

Her work is widely appreciated by those
who enjoy exploring the intricacies of life
and the world around us.

@UparimArt